Tunnels

Joanne Mattern

rourkeeducationalmedia.com

Scan for Related Titles
and Teacher Resources

Before Reading:

Building Academic Vocabulary and Background Knowledge

Before reading a book, it is important to tap into what your child or students already know about the topic. This will help them develop their vocabulary, increase their reading comprehension, and make connections across the curriculum.

1. *Look at the cover of the book. What will this book be about?*
2. *What do you already know about the topic?*
3. *Let's study the Table of Contents. What will you learn about in the book's chapters?*
4. *What would you like to learn about this topic? Do you think you might learn about it from this book? Why or why not?*
5. *Use a reading journal to write about your knowledge of this topic. Record what you already know about the topic and what you hope to learn about the topic.*
6. *Read the book.*
7. *In your reading journal, record what you learned about the topic and your response to the book.*
8. *After reading the book complete the activities below.*

Content Area Vocabulary
Read the list. What do these words mean?

ancient
bedrock
boring
concrete
conveyor
debris
engineers
explosives
maintenance
reservoirs
scaffold
transatlantic
ventilate

After Reading:

Comprehension and Extension Activity

After reading the book, work on the following questions with your child or students in order to check their level of reading comprehension and content mastery.

1. *Explain the differences and similarities between the tunnel-boring method and blasting method. (Summarize)*
2. *When reading the title, how did you picture it in your mind? (Visualizing)*
3. *When have you used tunnels? (Text to self connection)*
4. *Why is having a ventilation system in a tunnel important? (Asking questions)*
5. *How are tunnels beneficial? (Summarize)*

Extension Activity

Some tunnels were created by having two teams meet in the middle. You will need a piece of cardboard, a pen, and a partner to demonstrate how well you can communicate your location. Stand the cardboard upright and hold the top so it does not fall over. You and your partner will be on each side and need to write an X on your side. Now take turns describing the location of your X. Once you believe you've found your partner's tunnel draw a circle. Using the pen, carefully punch a hole through the cardboard. Did you meet the ends? How well were you able to communicate your location to your partner on the other side?

Table of Contents

JUN - - 2016

This low, narrow tunnel was built by ancient people called the Hittites using simple tools in what is now Turkey.

The First Tunnels

How do people get from one place to another? Sometimes there are obstacles that block the way, such as a mountain or a body of water. Thousands of years ago, **ancient engineers** came up with a way to cross these obstacles. They built a passageway under the ground. This passageway is called a tunnel.

We don't know who built the first tunnel, but we do know they have been used for at least 4,000 years. About that time, people known as Babylonians built a tunnel under the Euphrates River. This tunnel connected the royal palace and a temple.

The Euphrates River was an important feature of the ancient landscape, but it was also an obstacle to be crossed by the Babylonian people who lived along its shores.

The Babylonians and their neighbors, the Persians, lived in the desert. Living in the desert makes it hard to find water. The Babylonians and Persians built tunnels to solve this problem. These tunnels were called *qanat* or *kareez*. They carried water underground, bringing it from faraway rivers and lakes to the desert where people lived. One of these tunnels carried fresh water from the Euphrates River to the royal palace through a 2,953 foot (900 meter) long tunnel that was lined with bricks.

Experts think there are hundreds, maybe thousands, of big tunnels in Iran.

Brain Builder!

Babylon was a city in ancient Mesopotamia, in what is now Iraq. Persia is now known as Iran.

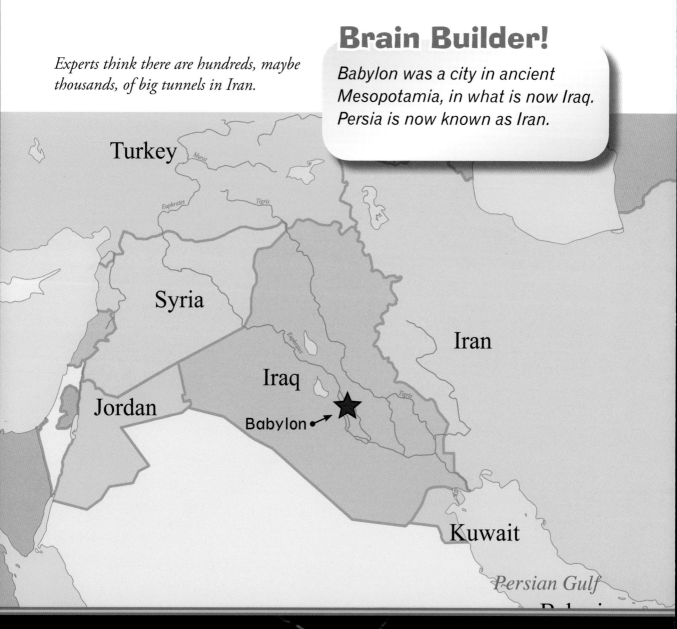

Gonabad

The city of Gonabad, Iran, still uses a network of qanat tunnels that is more than 2,700 years old. The qanats provide water to more than 40,000 people and also irrigates farmland.

This qanat is similar to those found in Gonabad, Iran. Like the Gonabad qanats, this tunnel was used to transport water for drinking and agriculture.

The ancient Greeks and Romans were also great tunnel builders. The Romans built more tunnels than any other ancient culture. Most of these tunnels were used to carry water from mountain streams down to the cities and villages.

*The Romans built this aqueduct, a tunnel designed to carry water, between ancient **reservoirs** known as Solomon's Pools and the city of Jerusalem sometime between 100 BCE and 30 BCE.*

In 36 BCE, the Romans built a tunnel in Italy between Naples and Pozzuoli that was 4,800 feet (1,463 meters) long, 25 feet (7.6 meters) wide, and 30 feet (9 meters) high. The tunnel was wide enough that two carts could pass each other inside it. This tunnel was dug through a hill. It was used until the 1800s, when more modern tunnels were built to replace it.

The tunnel built by ancient Romans between Naples and Puzzuoli was used for almost ▶ 2,000 years.

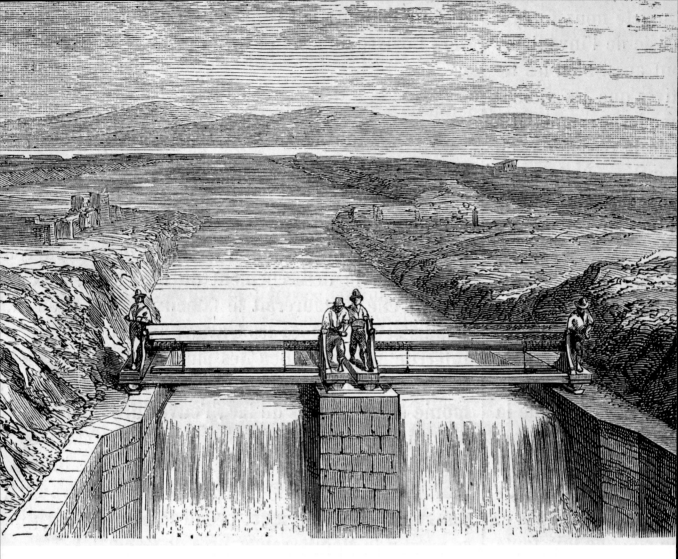

People drain lakes to provide more land for building or to control flooding. This drawing shows a water drainage system for Italy's Fucine Lake.

In 41 CE, 30,000 Roman men worked for 10 years to dig a tunnel to drain a lake named Lacus Fucinus. The tunnel was 3.5 miles (6 kilometers) long. First, the workers dug shafts that were up to 400 feet (122 meters) deep and 120 feet (36.5 meters) apart. Then, they dug through the rock to connect each shaft. To break through the rock, the Romans probably used a method called fire quenching. They heated the rock with fire and then cooled it with cold water. This sudden change in temperature made the rock crack and break off.

Most of the workers who built tunnels in ancient Rome were slaves. Thousands of these men died building tunnels. They were killed when the walls collapsed, or when there wasn't enough air to breathe far under the ground. The ancient Romans didn't pay much attention to safety since there were plenty more slaves to do the work.

This drawing shows slaves building an aqueduct through a mountain. Thousands of slaves lost their lives on tunnel projects in the ancient world. It was only much later that engineers came up with ways to keep their paid workers safe.

How Tunnels Work

Building a tunnel is one of the hardest challenges an engineer can face. That's because so many things can go wrong.

Tunnels are built through dirt or stone. The materials around them have a lot of weight. That weight presses down on the tunnel, which can cause it to collapse. A tunnel has to be very strong to stand this pressure.

Many tunnels are round. That's because a circle spreads the pressure evenly around the outside of the tunnel instead of focusing all the weight on one place. ▶

Another problem with digging tunnels is water. Water is present deep underground, and it rushes in when you dig a deep hole. People who design and build tunnels have to pump out the water and figure out how to keep water out of the tunnels while they are being built.

This photo of a tunnel-boring machine shows the wet, muddy conditions inside a tunnel.

Builders use special pumps to keep water out and fresh air in when they are building a tunnel. This building contains the ventilation system for a tunnel.

A third problem with tunnels is ventilation, or air flow. There isn't enough air to breathe when you are in a tunnel deep underground. There may also be dangerous gases deep in the Earth. In order to build a tunnel, engineers have to figure out how to **ventilate** it. They need to pump in fresh air and pump out carbon dioxide and other gases that can make it impossible to breathe.

The first step to building a tunnel is to figure out what kind of rock it will go through. Engineers study the soil and rock types in the area where the tunnel will be built. Some types of rock are harder than other types. Soil is much softer than rock and more likely to cave in.

Brain Builder!

The Thames Tunnel was the first tunnel dug under a major river since ancient times. Construction began in 1825 and the tunnel opened in 1843. People were so excited about the idea of a tunnel under the river that they called it "The Eighth Wonder of the World." On opening day, 50,000 people showed up, paid a penny, and walked through the new tunnel.

It is important for tunnel engineers to know what kind of soil they have to work with. This engineer is testing the soil to see what properties it has so the builders can plan the safest, easiest way to create their tunnel.

In 1825, a French engineer named Marc Isambard Brunel was working on a tunnel under the Thames River in London. Digging the tunnel was dangerous because the soft ground under the river could collapse at any moment. Brunel invented a tunnel shield to stop the soil from caving in. The shield was made of 12 connected frames covered by heavy plates. The shield pushed into the ground. Workers inside the shield then carved away the dirt and cleaned up any loose rocks or soil. Later, they built a permanent tunnel out of bricks that was strong enough to hold back the soil pressure.

This scale model of Marc Isambard Brunel's tunnel shield, exhibited at the Brunel Museum in Rotherhithe, England, shows how the engineer developed his machine to dig a tunnel under the soft soil of the Thames River in London.

Digging through dirt is hard enough, but how do construction workers dig through solid rock? There are several ways. One of the simplest methods to use is blasting with **explosives**. First workers build a **scaffold**, called a jumbo, and fill it with explosives. The jumbo is moved into the tunnel. Holes are drilled into the rock. An average hole is ten feet (3.05 meters) deep and a few inches wide. Next, workers pack the explosives into the holes. Then the workers leave the tunnel and detonate, or set off, the explosives by remote control. After the explosion, workers carry out the fallen rock and other materials on carts.

Workers use heavy equipment to carefully place explosives inside the rocks of a tunnel. After the dynamite is in place, they leave the area and the rocks are blasted away. This process is repeated along the length of the tunnel.

Blasting through rock is a long, slow process. Today, engineers use special machines called TBMs, or tunnel-**boring** machines, to drill through rock. TBMs are huge pieces of equipment with a round plate on one end. The plate is covered with sharp steel disks or steel-cutting teeth. As the plate slowly spins around, the disks and teeth cut into the rock. The broken bits of rock fall through spaces onto a **conveyor** system. The system carries the **debris** to the back of the machine, where workers take it away.

Modern tunnel-boring machines include a shield to support the tunnel as the machine bores through the rock.

How do you build a tunnel under water? First, a long hole called a trench is dug into the soil under the water. Then, long tubes made of steel or **concrete** are floated to the area and sunk into the trench. Each end of the tubes are sealed to keep out the water. Divers connect the tubes and remove the seals. Then any extra water is pumped out and the entire tunnel is covered with dirt.

Brain Builder!

There are three types of tunnels. Mine tunnels are used to pull mineral and metal deposits from deep inside the Earth. Public works tunnels carry water, gas, or sewage through cities and towns. Transportation tunnels carry cars and trains from one place to another.

Small trains carry workers and materials in and out of mines.

Trains move quickly in and out of a modern subway station in London.

Subways and Trains

As cities got bigger and more crowded, people needed a better way to get around. One way to solve this issue was to build tunnels under the ground where trains could carry passengers. These underground train lines are called subways.

A subway train runs through a tunnel under a London street.

The first subway in the world was built in London. It opened in 1863. The first line was only a little more than three miles (4.8 kilometers) long. Train locomotives pulled the cars, filling the tunnels with thick, black smoke.

The first subway in the United States opened in Boston in 1897. Just seven years later, on October 27, 1904, the New York City subway opened. Plans to build the subway began in 1900. At that time, most people got around using streetcars or elevated trains. The streets were very crowded, and it was difficult to get into downtown Manhattan from other parts of the city. The subway changed all of that.

In the early years of the 20th century, the streets of New York were filled with pedestrians, horses, and carts. Building the subway made it much easier to get around the crowded streets.

This drawing shows an early subway station at 23rd Street and 4th Avenue in New York City.

New York's subway tunnels were built under the streets wherever it was possible. The first part of the subway was built using a construction method called cut-and-cover. The street was dug up and workers built the tunnel. Once the tunnel was finished, workers rebuilt the street on top of it. Other tunnels were drilled through rock and built under rivers. Today, the New York City subway has 468 stations, more than any other subway system in the world. It has 842 miles (1,355 kilometers) of track and carried 1.71 billion passengers in 2013.

It was easy to dig up the streets, but some of New York's subways had to travel under rivers. Workers built a heavy frame with a roof to support the tunnel as they built it.

Second Avenue Subway

The New York City subway is growing even bigger. In 2007, construction began on the Second Avenue Subway. This time, though, workers aren't digging up the city streets. Giant machines drill the tunnel underground without affecting the streets and buildings above. It is expected to be complete by December 2016.

Once completed, the Second Avenue subway will be New York City's first major expansion of the subway system in more than 50 years. This photo shows the underground world of the 86th Street Station under construction.

Trains use tunnels too. The Seikan Tunnel is the longest and deepest railway tunnel in the world. It runs under the Tsugaru Strait between the Japanese islands of Honshu and Hokkaido. Traveling across the strait by boat was very difficult because of the many storms and rough conditions. To solve this problem, Japanese engineers started to plan a railway tunnel back in the 1930s. However, construction did not start until 1971.

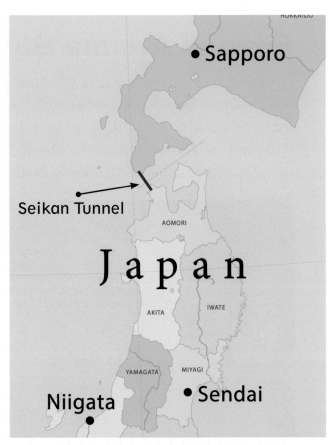

Longest Railway Tunnels		
Tunnel Name	**Country**	**Length**
1. Seikan Tunnel	Japan	33.46 miles / 53.85 km
2. Channel Tunnel	England	31.4 miles / 50.4 km
3. Lotschberg Base Tunnel	Switzerland	21.5 miles / 34.6 km
4. Guadarrama Rail Tunnel	Spain	17.6 miles / 28.4 km
5. Taihang Tunnel	China	17.27 miles / 27.8 km
6. Hakkoda Tunnel	Japan	16.43 miles / 26.45 km
7. Iwate-Ichinohe Tunnel	Japan	16 miles / 25.81 km
8. Daishimizu Tunnel	Japan	13.67 miles / 22 km
9. Wushaoling Tunnel	China	13.08 miles / 21.05 km
10. Geumjeong Tunnel	South Korea	12.6 miles / 20.3 km

Japan's Seikan Tunnel is 1,115 feet (340 meters) below the surface of the water and just over 33 miles (54 kilometers) long. It took 16 years to build.

First of all, workers had to dig through cracked, weak rock with water leaking in. To solve this problem, workers blasted out the rock with explosives. Then, they drilled holes in the tunnel walls and filled them with cement. The cement made the walls stronger and kept out water. The tunnel opened in 1988.

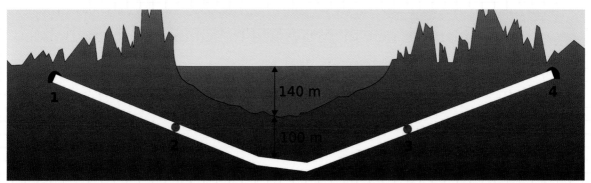

(1) Honshū end (2) Tappi-Kaitei Station (3) Yoshioka-Kaitei Station (4) Hokkaidō end.

Completed in 1927, the Holland Tunnel was the first tunnel to link New Jersey and New York City, making it possible for people to live farther away from their jobs in the city.

Underwater Highways

Cars and trucks use tunnels too. Before the 1920s, most people used horses or carriages to get around. By the 1920s, cars had become so popular that new highways had to be built for them. Builders also needed to create ways for cars and trucks to cross bodies of water. That meant more tunnels had to be built as well.

The Holland Tunnel opened in 1927. This tunnel travels under the Hudson River and connects New Jersey to New York City. The Holland Tunnel is 1.6 miles (2.6 kilometers) long and contains two tubes built into the **bedrock** at the bottom of the river. Each tube carries two lanes of traffic on a 20 foot (6 meter) wide roadway. About 100,000 vehicles travel through the Holland Tunnel every day.

Drivers enter the Holland Tunnel on the west side of Manhattan Island, then exit at the eastern edge of New Jersey.

This photo of the Holland Tunnel under construction shows the curved shape that helps make the tunnel stronger.

The people who built the Holland Tunnel came up with a clever way to keep water out. During construction, both ends of the tunnel were sealed and air was pumped inside. The high pressure of the air kept the river water out of the tunnel.

Brain Builder!

Car tunnels, such as the Holland Tunnel, also require a system for getting rid of carbon monoxide. This deadly gas is in the exhaust produced by cars and trucks. To keep everyone in the Holland Tunnel safe, 84 fans create a constant airflow through the tunnel. These fans can completely change all of the air inside the tunnel every 90 seconds.

Ventilation units are housed in four towers that are part of the Holland Tunnel.

Drivers in the Mont Blanc Tunnel travel deep under the Alps. This tunnel is the deepest in the world.

The Mont Blanc Tunnel is another famous tunnel used by vehicles. This tunnel connects Chamonix, France, with Courmayeur, Italy. To do this, the tunnel runs underneath Mont Blanc, the highest mountain in the Alps, a famous mountain range in Europe.

The Mont Blanc Tunnel opened in 1965. It is just over seven miles (11 kilometers) long and has a two-lane roadway that is 23 feet (7 meters) wide. Five engineers and 350 workers built the tunnel. They used more than 772 tons (700 metric tons) of explosives to blast through the strong rock. The workers were split into two teams. One team worked from France to Italy. The other team worked from Italy to France. When they met in the middle, the tunnel was finished.

Tunnel Tragedy

In 1999, there was a fire inside the Mont Blanc Tunnel. Thirty-nine people died. The tunnel was closed for three years while it was improved. Now that it's reopened, security cameras watch everything inside the tunnel, and firefighters are on duty 24 hours a day.

Thousands of cars travel through the Mont Blanc Tunnel every day.

Linking Countries

Tunnels don't just link cities and towns. They also can connect one country to another. These types of tunnels face special challenges.

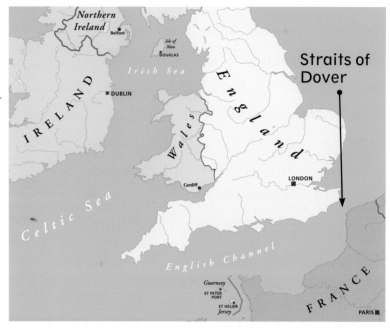

The English Channel is a narrow body of water that separates England and France. At its narrowest point, called the Straits of Dover, the Channel is 22 miles (35.4 kilometers) wide. For centuries, the only way to cross those 22 miles was by boat. People in both countries knew there had to be a better way.

Someone standing on the beach in France can see England across the water, but it wasn't until the Channel Tunnel was completed in 1994 that crossing the English Channel became an easy trip.

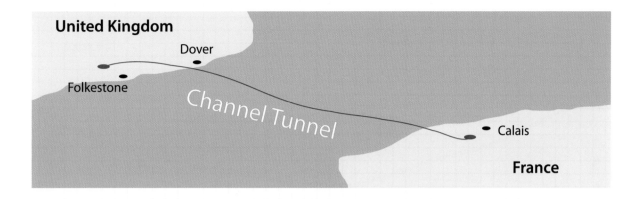

Plans for a channel tunnel go back as far as 1802. However, it wasn't until 1984 that the governments of the two countries agreed to build a tunnel. Construction started in 1987. One construction crew started digging in England and another crew started digging in France. The project used huge TBMs that could cut through about 750 feet (228.60 meters) of rock a day. Extra heavy, waterproof concrete liners were installed inside the tunnel walls to hold back the water and prevent the tunnel from collapsing from the force of the water pressure. Then, curved sheets of steel were installed inside the concrete to make the inside walls of the tunnel.

Construction crews from England and France celebrate as they meet in the middle of the English Channel. The project used satellites to pinpoint the location of each tunnel so they would line up correctly.

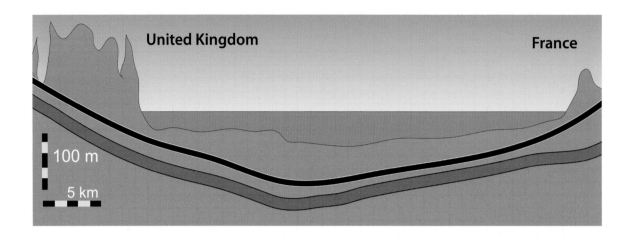

United Kingdom　　　　　　　　　　　France

100 m

5 km

The Channel Tunnel, or Chunnel, was finished in 1994. It was the second-longest underwater tunnel in the world and the longest tunnel between two countries. The Channel Tunnel also has the longest undersea section.

Cars line up inside a train traveling through the Channel Tunnel. Up to 400 trains travel through the tunnel each day.

24 teur avant le début du débarquement.

The Channel Tunnel is actually three tunnels. Two main tunnels carry trains. Between these tunnels is a smaller service tunnel. This tunnel carries **maintenance** workers and equipment. It also provides an emergency exit.

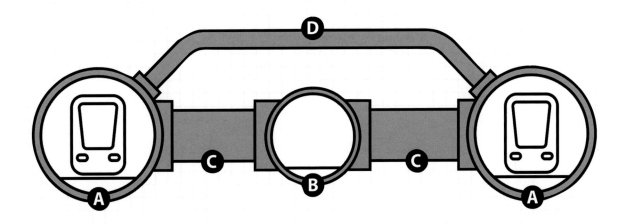

A: Train tunnel
B: Service tunnel kept at higher air pressure to prevent smoke/fumes entering
C: Cross passage/Evacuation walkway
D: Duct to equalize tunnel air pressure

Channel Tunnel by the Numbers

31.4 miles (50.4 kilometers) total length of tunnel

24 miles (38 kilometers)   length of undersea part of tunnel

24.9 feet (7.6 meters)   width of each rail tunnel

15.7 feet (4.8 meters)   width of service tunnel

29.5 feet (9 meters)   width of largest TBMs used on the project

1,650 tons (1,500 metric tons)   weight of largest TBMs used

Tunnel under construction

Tunnels of the Future

Tunnels have been built in many places and in many ways. People will continue to build tunnels in the future. What will these tunnels look like? We don't know yet, but one thing is for sure: The tunnels of the future likely will be longer than anything built today.

The Trans-Siberian Railway crosses Russia and includes more than 40 tunnels.

A tunnel project in Switzerland will soon break a record. The Gotthard Base Tunnel will be 35 miles (57 kilometers) long, which is longer than the Seikan Tunnel in Japan. The Gotthard Base Tunnel, which runs through the Swiss Alps, will be part of a new high-speed rail link between the cities of Zurich, Switzerland, and Milan, Italy. Work began in 1996 and the tunnel is expected to open in 2016.

Workers wave the Swiss flag in celebration after drilling through rock at the final section of the Gotthard Base Tunnel.

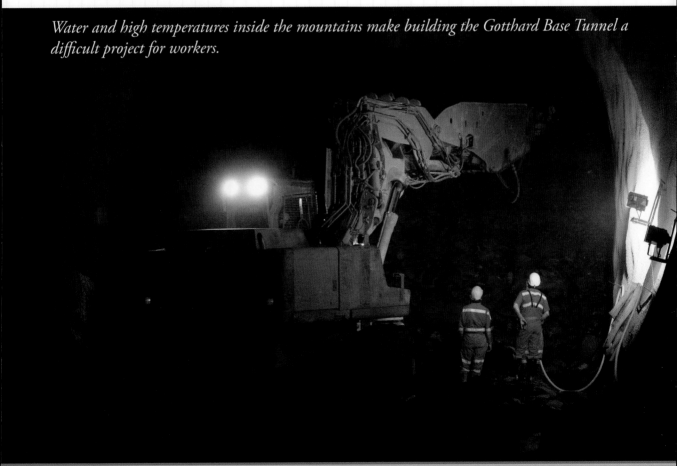

Water and high temperatures inside the mountains make building the Gotthard Base Tunnel a difficult project for workers.

Many people would like to build a tunnel between Alaska in the United States to Russia. The two countries are only about 55 miles (88.51 kilometers) apart. Engineers say that up to 99 million tons (90 million metric tons) of freight could be carried through a tunnel connecting Alaska and Russia.

In 2011, the Russian government gave the go-ahead to plan this project. However, like most engineering projects, this kind of tunnel would be expensive – about $65 billion.

Russia

Alaska and Russia are separated by a body of water called the Bering Strait.

Alaska

Bering
Strait

Engineers are even thinking of building a tunnel across the Atlantic Ocean! This tunnel would link Europe and the United States. The tunnel would use high-speed magnetic trains that could travel up to 4,970 miles (8,000 kilometers) an hour. If a train traveled at that speed, it would take just over an hour to travel from London, England, to New York City.

A **transatlantic** tunnel would be 215 times longer than Japan's Seikan Tunnel, and it would cost at least $12 trillion to build. This project won't be built anytime soon. But as technology gets better, there is no telling what the future may bring.

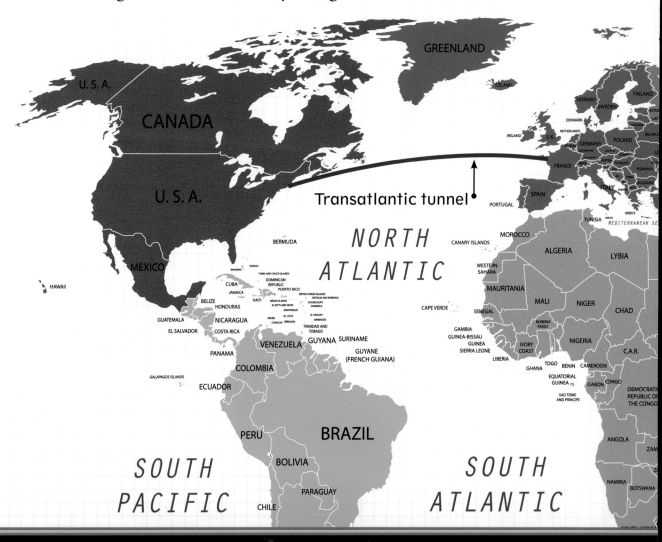

Brain Builder!

Modern engineers aren't the first people to think of a tunnel across the Atlantic Ocean. In 1935, a science fiction movie called The Tunnel *was based on this idea. Of course, the characters faced many obstacles, including an underwater volcano, but end up building the tunnel after all.*

Technology is always changing and improving. In the future, it might be possible to build a tunnel across the Atlantic Ocean, a distance of about 3,455 miles (5,576 kilometers).

RUSSIA

KAZAKHSTAN

MONGOLIA

CASPIAN SEA

UZBEKISTAN

KYRGYZSTAN

TURKMENISTAN

TAJIKISTAN

NORTH KOREA

JAPAN

IRAQ

IRAN

AFGHANISTAN

CHINA

SOUTH KOREA

KUWAIT

PAKISTAN

NORTH PACIFIC

BAHRAIN

QATAR

SAUDI ARABIA

U.A.E.

NEPAL

BHUTAN

INDIA

TAIWAN

OMAN

MYANMAR (BURMA)

BANGLADESH

ERITREA

YEMEN

THAILAND

LAOS

NORTHERN MARIANA ISLANDS

PHILIPPINES

DJIBOUTI

CAMBODIA

VIETNAM

GUAM

SOMALIA

ETHIOPIA

PALAU

MARSHALL ISLANDS

MICRONESIA

SRI LANKA

BRUNEI

MALDIVES

MALAYSIA

KENYA

SEYCHELLES

SINGAPORE

MALAYSIA

PAPUA NEW GUINEA

NAURU

RWANDA

INDIAN

INDONESIA

BURUNDI

SOLOMON ISLANDS

COMOROS

EAST TIMOR

TUVALU

MAYOTTE

OCEAN

MALAWI

MADAGASCAR

MAURITIUS

VANUATU

FIJI

AMERICAN SAMOA

MOZAMBIQUE

REUNION

NEW CALEDONIA

TONGA

AUSTRALIA

Timeline

circa 2000 BCE - Babylonians build a tunnel under the Euphrates River.

circa 700 BCE - Qanat tunnels are built in Gonabad, Iran.

36 BCE - Ancient Romans build a tunnel between Naples and Pozzuoli.

41 CE - Ancient Romans build a tunnel to drain Lacus Fucinus.

1825 - Marc Isambard Brunel invents the tunnel shield.

1843 - The Thames Tunnel opens in London, England.

1863 - The world's first subway opens in London.

1897 - The first subway in the United States opens in Boston.

1904 - The New York City subway opens.

1927 - The Holland Tunnel opens linking New York City and New Jersey.

1965 - The Mont Blanc Tunnel opens in the Alps.

1988 - The Seikan Tunnel opens in Japan.

1994 - The Channel Tunnel opens between England and France.

1999 - A fire in the Mont Blanc Tunnel kills 39 people.

2007 - Construction begins on the Second Avenue Subway in New York City.

2016 - The Gotthard Base Tunnel is expected to open in Switzerland, becoming the longest railway tunnel in the world.

Glossary

ancient (AYN-shuhnt): belonging to the distant past

bedrock (BED-ROK): the rock at the bottom of a body of water

boring (BORE-ing): drilling a hole through rock

concrete (KON-kreet): a building material made from sand, gravel, cement, and water

conveyor (kuhn-VAY-ur): a moving belt that carries objects from one place to another

debris (duh-BREE): pieces of something that has been broken

engineers (en-juhn-NEERZ): people who design construction projects

explosives (ek-SPLOH-sivs): things that can blow up

maintenance (MAYN-tuh-nuhns): the process of keeping something in good condition by checking and repairing it

reservoirs (REZ-ur-vwahrs); natural or artificial lakes in which water is collected and stored

scaffold (SKAF-uhld): a framework of wooden planks that workers stand on

transatlantic (tranz-at-LAN-tik): crossing the Atlantic Ocean

ventilate (VEN-tuh-late): to allow fresh air into a place and let stale air out

Index

Show What You Know

1. What is the longest tunnel in the world and where is it located?
2. In what year did the Holland Tunnel open?
3. How long will the Gotthard Base Tunnel be when it is complete?
4. What is one problem that occurs when digging tunnels in water?
5. Who invented the tunnel shield?

Websites to Visit

www.pbs.org/wgbh/buildingbig/tunnel

wonderopolis.org/wonder/how-do-you-build-a-tunnel-underwater

www.sciencekids.co.nz/sciencefacts/engineering/tunnels.html

About the Author

Joanne Mattern has written hundreds of books for children. Her favorite subjects are history, nature, sports, and biographies. She enjoys traveling around the United States and visiting new places. Joanne grew up on the banks of the Hudson River in New York State and still lives in the area with her husband, four children, and numerous pets.

Meet The Author!
www.meetREMauthors.com

www.rourkeeducationalmedia.com

PHOTO CREDITS: Cover © iWorkAlong; title page © captainflash; page 4 © Giancana; page 5 © Joel Carillet; page 7 ©NAEINSUN; page 8, 29, 31 © Library of Congress; page 9 © Armondo mancini; page 10 © marolino; page 11 © DEA Picture Library/gettyimages.com; page 12 © ollirg; page 13 © Panagiotis Karpanagiotis; page 14 © Karem Kurluva; page 15 © Kropic; page 16 © Keithfrithkeith; page 17 © Duncan Kimbal; page 19 © Holger Ellagaard; page 20 © Matatu; page 21 © Tomas Sereda; page 22 © urbancow, Uwe Zänker; page 23 © Strohmeyer and Wyman/Library of Congress, Courtesy of NYC Municipal Archives; page 24 © Courtesy of NYC Municipal Archives; page 25 © Metroploitan Transportation Authority/Patrick Cashin; page 26 © Frank Ramspott; page 27 © Ariake, Commander Keane; page 28 © Anna Bryukhanove; page 30 © University Archives/University of Illionois at Urbana-Champaign; page 32 © Focusphoto; page 33 © Costa007; page 34 © Creative Nature; page 35 © experimental, AP; page 36 © experimental, Hornpipe; page 38 © ollo, asafta; page 39 © AP/Christain Hartmann, gettyimges.com/ Johannes Simon

Edited by: Keli Sipperley

Cover and interior design by: Renee Brady

Library of Congress PCN Data

Tunnels / Joanne Mattern
(Engineering Wonders)
ISBN 978-1-63430-420-7 (hard cover)
ISBN 978-1-63430-520-4 (soft cover)
ISBN 978-1-63430-611-9 (e-Book)
Library of Congress Control Number: 2015931734

Printed in the United States of America, North Mankato, Minnesota

Also Available as:
ROURKE'S
e-Books